LIFE IS NOT ABOUT *finding yourself* IT IS ABOUT *creating yourself*

life is a gift when you embrace the present

knowing is a gift of confidence in our choices

a butterfly will never see the beauty of its wings and yet it graces the sky

CREATIVITY HELPS US SHINE BRIGHT

from every negative comes the potential for a positive outcome

Everyone has a story to share

SET AN INTENTION & THINGS WILL ALIGN

JOURNALING helps clear our minds

Pause on the journey it will be more fulfilling

it is only when you have the right key that the RIGHT DOOR will unlock

learn everyday, for there is something new to learn in every day.

do everything with love

light the lamp to **BRIGHTEN** the path of someone lost

There is *strength* in *gentleness*

love is the greatest POWER one that has LASTING EFFECT

make time to be CREATIVE

small steps combined equal BIG goals

to give your best to others you must first give your best to you today is the to make that choice

When opportunity knocks push the door ajar

WHERE THERE IS A WILL THERE IS ALWAYS A WAY

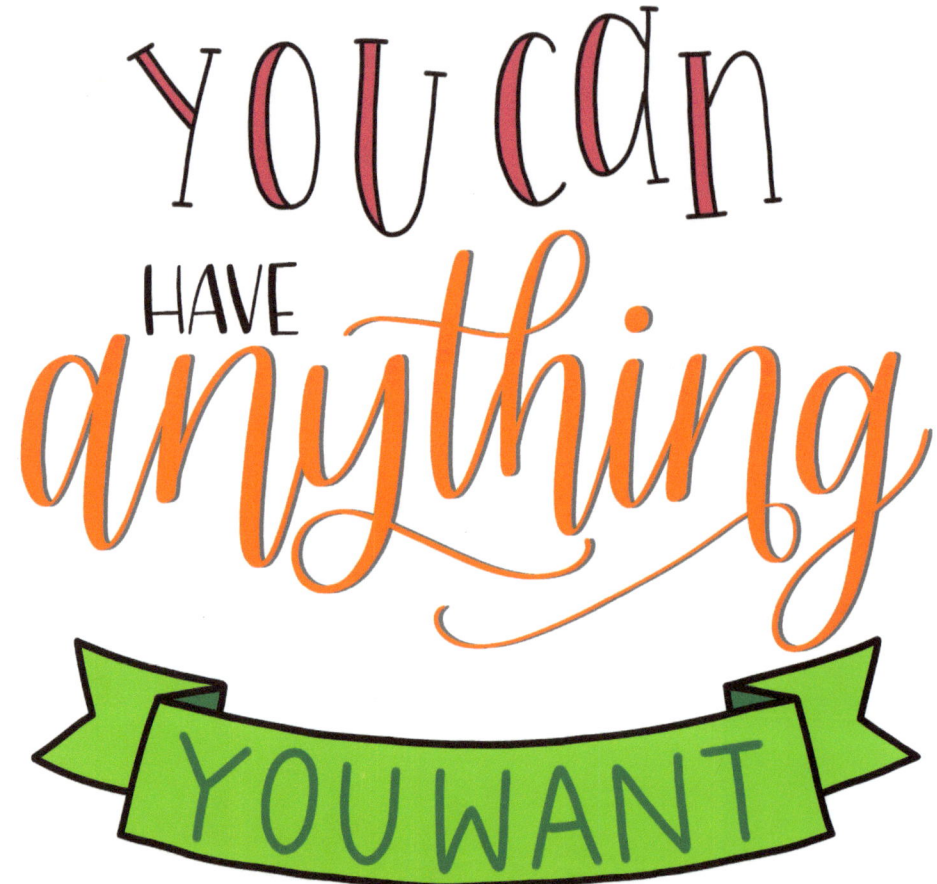

SURROUND YOURSELF WITH THOSE WHO UPLIFT YOU

The GREATEST gift is to EMBRACE WHO YOU ARE NOW & WHO YOU WANT TO become in the future

about the illustrator

Chelsea Wilcox is a hand lettering specialist. Her passion for making words beautiful is a sought after talent and a gift to the world.

Originally from Reading, UK and now residing in Perth, Western Australia she shares her creative talent across the globe, a goal she is focused on building her future portfolio upon.

You can find Chelsea online at Instagram @art.cw20

about the author

Karen McDermott is an award-winning publisher, author and advanced Law of Attraction practitioner.
Having published many journals, fiction, non-fiction books and children's books Karen was delighted to team up with the talented Chelsea Wilcox to bring her inspiring words to life in special lettering.
You can find Karen online at Serenity Press, Making Magic Happen Press and Karen Mc Dermott.com.au.
Facebook @mmhpress @serenitypress Instagram @mmhpress & @karenmcdermott

Copyright © 2019 Karen Mc Dermott

Illustrations © Chelsea Wilcox

Published by Making Magic Happen Press,

Perth, WA.

www.mmhpress.com.

All rights reserved. No part of this book may be used or reproduced in any manner whatsoever withour prior written consent of the author, except as provided by the Australian copyright law.

National Library of Australia Cataloguing-in-Publisher data:

Non- Fiction : inspirational

ISBN (hc) 978-0-6485123-0-1

ISBN (sc) 978-0-6485378-2-3

Printed on sustainable paper.

www.ingramcontent.com/pod-product-compliance
Lightning Source LLC
Chambersburg PA
CBHW042147290426
44110CB00003B/138